FIFTY YEARS OF SOVIET FOREIGN POLICY

Studies in International Affairs Number 6

Studies in International Affairs Number 6

FIFTY YEARS OF SOVIET FOREIGN POLICY

by Herbert S. Dinerstein

The Washington Center of Foreign Policy Research
School of Advanced International Studies
The Johns Hopkins University

The Johns Hopkins Press, Baltimore, Maryland

To my wife, Rita

FOREWORD

The simpler, more intense phases of the predominately bipolar cold war have now given way to a more complicated American-Soviet relationship within an increasingly pluralistic pattern of international politics. Yet—as at the beginning of the cold war twenty years ago—the two superpowers remain militarily preponderant, and their relations are still a dominant factor in all the major conflicts and alignments in the world. This may hold true for a long time—even for another twenty years. On the other hand, American and Soviet policies will surely change substantially as each state reacts to the other's efforts to adjust familiar policies to unfamiliar circumstances.

To understand this interaction it is essential to see it in historical perspective. On the Soviet side it is useful to look backward fifty years—to the Bolshevik revolution—so as to include the formative period of Soviet (as distinguished from Russian) foreign policy when relations with the United States were relatively unimportant (just as it is useful to go back to at least the beginning of the twentieth century to comprehend the roots of America's policy as a world power). In this essay Professor Dinerstein interprets the changing Soviet-American interaction since World War II in the light of fifty years of Soviet foreign policy and focuses his analysis on recent developments with crucial implications for the future.

This is the sixth title to be published in our Studies in International Affairs Series. The Series is designed to provide a medium-length publications format for analyses of current issues in international politics.

December, 1967   ROBERT E. OSGOOD
Director
Washington Center of
Foreign Policy Research

CONTENTS

FIFTY YEARS OF SOVIET FOREIGN POLICY

Studies in International Affairs Number 6

I. INTRODUCTION

It may be useful fifty years after the founding of the Soviet State to review its foreign policy in order to define its motive forces and to determine if and how any of these have changed. The purpose of this essay is to examine only some of the features of Soviet foreign policy; it is not intended to provide a synoptic history.

It was not until 1921 that the new regime knew that it had bested its internal and external enemies. At first the leaders of the new state doubted that it could last without the political and economic support of other socialist states in industrialized countries. Somewhat to their surprise, however, the Soviet Union was able to survive on its own, if only just barely. By contrast, the Soviet Union is now one of the older established states of the world. In Europe, apart from the Scandinavian countries, Switzerland, and Great Britain, no other government has held power continuously for as long. France, Germany, Italy, all the states of central and eastern Europe, and the Balkans have not enjoyed continuity of government in this period. The Soviet Union is not only a senior and the greatest power in Europe, but also one of the two world powers. The only Socialist state in 1917, the Soviet Union is now part of a system, albeit a disintegrating system, of socialist states.

Despite her size, Russia had been too weak to enter the first rank of great powers. In the brief span of half a century, however, the newly formed Soviet Union entered the first rank of powers. Even the most doctrinaire beliefs and the most rigid practices have to be accommodated to such a radical change in the power of a state. How these doctrines and practices have changed is the subject of this essay.

The process of change has been complex, influenced by the developing international position of the Soviet Union, internal political fluctuations, and its changing perception of the outside world. Since Soviet perception of the outside world has centered largely on changing appraisals of the United States, more attention than is customary has been devoted to the American political scene on the assumption that it has provided a major ingredient in the development of Soviet foreign policy.

Two themes have been selected for extended treatment: first, the replacement of the belief in temporary coexistence by the belief in the possibility of extended coexistence; second, the existence of mutual misperception. It is important at the outset to clarify what is meant by the latter. I do not mean to imply that the interests of the Soviet Union and those of its main opponents, particularly the United States, were largely compatible and that it was willful or doctrinaire failure to discern the opportunities for accommodation that made relations worse than they had to be. On the contrary, the Soviet expectation that the tide of human affairs was running against the capitalists and that it was their duty to augment the strength of that tide, when feasible and not too risky, predetermined hostility and tension as long as the United States believed that only its opposition could prevent Soviet success.

I do not mean to accept as valid the familiar and simplistic thesis that, were it not for some misunderstandings derived from ill-will and ignorance, Soviet-American relations would have been reasonably untroubled. Very often, in fact, high tension was the product of a clear-cut mutual understanding of the conflict of interests. Both sides, for example, believed that the establishment of missile bases in Cuba would significantly alter the strategic equation; both sides understood that changes in the political arrangements for West Berlin would significantly alter the balance of forces in Europe; and around these two issues the two major powers confronted each other most dramatically in the postwar period. However, misperception has played an important role in the foreign policy of the Soviet Union. Three forms of misperception stand out: Without assessment of them, an understanding of the international relations of the Soviet Union is incomplete.

1. Taking an opponent's ideological pronouncements as a sufficient guide to his future conduct is the first cause of misperception. Proponents of communist doctrine expect that as the historical process unfolds, capitalism will disappear, and they enjoin the socialist states and the revolutionary forces within the capitalist world to hasten that process at the appropriate times and places. If capitalist statesmen neglect the last qualifying phrase in an obsessive desire to anticipate and forestall every possible threat, they do not allow for communist decisions to withdraw temporarily or to accept the status quo for a time. Communist ideological statements play both a ritual and an internal political role, and failure to accord each its proper place creates false estimates. Similarly, Western ideological pronouncements are taken at face value by communist analysts. The "roll back" slogan of the 1952 election campaign worried communist leaders. To add that such an assessment provided political justification for policies already adopted in eastern Europe and in the Soviet Union helps explain why that judgment was so

readily made, but the fact remains that the root of the misapprehension lay in taking ideological rhetoric at face value.

2. A second class of misperception is derived from the speed and manner with which each side adjusted to the radical changes in weapons technology and the power balance. In both countries established military leaders, whose careers were associated with traditional weapons, resisted the conclusion that nuclear weapons had reduced other arms to secondary importance if not to redundancy. Effective opposition to change lasted longer in the Soviet Union, primarily because nuclear weapons were acquired later but also because of the essentially more conservative character of Soviet society. Although the timing was different, both countries reached the same conclusion: only a direct threat to national survival could justify a resort to war. From this sobering reflection different political conclusions were drawn. The Soviet leaders could no longer believe that war was inevitable as long as capitalism existed because that meant that to all intents and purposes socialism was doomed. The two theories of the inevitability of war and the ultimate triumph of socialism were incompatible and, not surprisingly, the first of these theories was retired. The United States had to choose between the fear that a nuclear war would end civilization and the conviction that any coincidence of Soviet and American interests was necessarily temporary because the goal of world communism was the star by which the Soviet state steered. Again it is not surprising that the second notion, not the first, was rejected. It is hardly necessary to elaborate on how profoundly these theoretical changes affected the political assumptions on which both societies operated.

Subordinate to this second class of misperception is the different understanding that each side had, at somewhat different times, of the relative strength of each other's power. It was generally assumed that the almost simultaneous acquisition of nuclear weapons by the Soviet Union and the United States would compress the time otherwise required for the Soviet Union to become equal in power to the United States. As events proved, however, nuclear weapons tended to cancel each other out, and the economic and political factors emerged as determinant. If economic and political strength is the measure, the Soviet Union and the United States can be equated only in the sense that they are the two greatest powers; but in any other sense the disparity in present power, as well as in potential, does not permit their assignment to the same class. Nevertheless, for several years both sides assumed a bipolar future world. The falsity of this assumption was not apprehended simultaneously nor in the same mood by both principals. Until its dissipation this illusion distorted mutual understanding.

3. A third factor distorting mutual understanding was each side's failure to comprehend the complexity of the other's decision-making. The deficiency in analysis derived mainly from an underestimation of the influence internal politics exercises over the formation of foreign policy. In the United States the idea of a monolithic Soviet Union in which all important matters were decided by the dictator dominated academic analysis for some time after it had much justification and colored official analysis even longer, perhaps to this day. In the Soviet case, a crude paradigm of the forces at play in American politics persisted into the late fifties. The underestimation of the complexity of each society, particularly of the domestic component of foreign policy, reinforced the tendency of each to judge the opponent on the basis of his ideological pronouncements.

The influence of domestic political-interest groups in

the Soviet Union can be usefully described by a U-curve with one point located in the 1920s, the trough from the middle 1930s to Stalin's death, and the second point from then until the present. It took Stalin longer to consolidate his dictatorship than is generally believed. The death of Kirov in December, 1934, marked the beginning of the last phase of consolidation. By March, 1938, with the termination of wholesale purges of the party and the governmental bureaucracy, Stalin was the undisputed master of the communist party and the supreme ruler of the Soviet Union. But during the twenties and most likely during part of the thirties he was fighting a battle against various oppositions within the party. Excellent accounts of that contest are available, and we shall confine ourselves to its implications for foreign policy.

The Soviet leadership was in agreement on very general propositions, such as the superiority of socialism over capitalism and the inevitable replacement of the latter by the former. But agreement on such general principles is of little value in determining what course to follow in particular instances. On almost every question of significance various theories flourished. Could socialism survive in one country? Was Europe on the brink of a new revolutionary wave in 1919, or was it not? Were Western capitalist leaders war-weary enough and sufficiently distracted by colonial revolts to break off the intervention? Had the danger of war increased so sharply in 1928, as was officially pronounced, that rapid industrialization had become an urgent necessity? Was it likely that the Soviet Union would need greater military power to protect her eastern borders against Japan? How far should the first Five Year Plan be altered to meet this new danger?

Marxism-Leninism hardly offered unequivocal an-

swers to this list of questions, which could easily be
extended. Obviously responses to these external chal-
lenges would have profound implications for the internal policies of the Soviet Union. And it was impossible
to consider these issues as isolated factors. In the Soviet
Union as elsewhere, judgments of the external danger
are influenced by attitudes toward domestic consequences.* The influence of domestic and foreign policies on each other took different forms. Sometimes
judgment of an external situation would be subtly and
indirectly influenced by an awareness of its implications for internal policy; at other times judgment of an
external situation would be crudely manipulated to justify a preferred internal policy. Sometimes the internal
issue at stake was broadly conceived, the pace of industrialization, for example. At other times the internal
issue was more narrowly drawn, discrediting a particular faction within the Politbureau or the dominant
leadership.

The interrelationship of domestic and foreign considerations disappeared from Soviet political life when
the purges of the thirties eliminated opposition. The
replacements for the party leaders and officials of the
twenties and thirties, who had often had direct experience abroad, were younger, more provincial men, who
were selected precisely because they had no pronounced views on domestic or foreign policy. In any
case, even if they had any strong preferences, the recent bloody purges had demonstrated how dangerous
it was to voice them. This group of men served as the

---

* An analogy with the United States at present could be
drawn. The "hards" on the Vietnamese war consider investment
in the poverty program as less urgent than the "softs" or, to put
it in another way, they have different estimates of the domestic
costs of the war.

agency for the execution of Stalin's policies and to a large extent for those of his successors. As a group they are limited in outlook, unventuresome, and deeply conservative. Their monopoly of all but the highest post meant that in the postwar period Stalin established the goals of Soviet foreign policy and prescribed the means for their execution, free from the hurly-burly of the factional politics of the upper levels of the communist party of an earlier period. The style he employed will be examined when we deal with the postwar foreign policy of the Soviet Union.

SOVIET FOREIGN POLICY UNTIL THE END OF WORLD WAR II

The Soviet state started its existence by fighting off the intervention of more than a dozen capitalist states and by defending itself against attacks from all four points of the compass. The desperate nature of the struggle and the narrow margin by which victory was won left an indelible imprint on the Soviet mind: the capitalists had once tried to throttle the Soviet Union and might well do so again, given a suitable combination of circumstances. Soviet historical accounts are naturally full of the heroism of the defenders and the brilliance of their strategy; but the more scholarly accounts realize that the intervention was halfhearted. The intervening powers were often at cross-purposes, and within the major powers organized labor mounted an effective opposition to a continuation of the intervention. As early as November, 1920, a formula for solitary survival was enunciated by Lenin: "So long as we remain, from the economic and military standpoint, weaker than the capitalist world, so long we must stick to the rule: we must be clever enough to utilize the contradictions and oppositions among the imperialists. . . . Politically we must utilize the conflicts among our adversaries which are explained by the most profound economic causes."[*]

In the first years after the departure of the armies of the interventionist powers, the Soviet Union pursued

[*] Lenin, *Sochineniia* [Works], XXV, 498, 501 as quoted in Edward Hallett Carr, *The Bolshevik Revolution, 1917–1923* (London, 1953), III, 276.

the policy of playing one capitalist power against another, mainly by supporting those who had suffered
from the peace settlements following World War I.
The Germans felt with considerable justice that the
Treaty of Versailles had been unduly punitive, and despite ideologic revulsion they understood that the Soviet connection could be exploited to press the Entente
Powers to modify the Treaty's terms. When the Bol-
sheviks concluded the first treaty with Germany at Ra-
pallo in 1922, they realized that the Germans were
using them to get better terms from the victorious Entente powers; but they were quite willing to be so used
because it "aggravated the contradictions of capitalism." The Soviet Union pursued the same policy toward the Turkey of Mustapha Kemal, which enjoyed
more rapid success in modifying the terms of the Treaty
of Sèvres than the Germans did in modifying the Treaty
of Versailles. Here Russian help was of more importance because the contesting forces were more evenly
balanced. The Anglo–French rivalry, evident enough in
policy-conflict over Germany, expressed itself in the
Near East in the British support for the Greeks (who
were endeavoring to force the Treaty of Sèvres on the
Turks) and the French support for the Turks. Soviet
assistance to Turkey was perhaps critical because at
some points the contest was so closely drawn that the
modest military assistance of which the Soviet Union
was capable could influence the outcome.

During this period of the coexistence of capitalism
and socialism, the Soviet leaders believed the general
trend favored the latter. Capitalism would become
weaker as colonies like India, or semicolonies like Turkey and China, threw off the imperialist yoke, depriv-
ing capitalist countries of the surplus profits that Lenin
had analyzed as being essential to their economies. In-

ternecine capitalist wars would also contribute to the deterioration of the system and, although particular wars could not be predicted, the phenomenon was accepted as a law of Marxism. Meanwhile the Soviet Union would grow stronger internally, thus fulfilling the prediction that socialism would wax as capitalism waned. This general prediction, however, allowed for temporary setbacks and reversals—and war with a major power was considered as such because, given the relative weakness of the Soviet Union, defeat was more likely than victory.

Soviet theory accepted the possibility that capitalist states might be torn apart by their internecine and internal struggles without making a war against the Soviet Union, but they believed it unlikely that world socialism would be attained so easily. They thought it likely that they would be involved in war sooner or later with capitalist countries, but wanted to postpone that fateful day as long as possible.

Neutrality in a capitalist war would be advantageous for the Soviet Union not only because capitalist countries would damage each other, thus enhancing the relative strength of the Soviet Union, but also because of the expected revolutionary consequences. Most historians would share the communist analysis that the dislocations of World War I made the Russian Revolution possible. Germany suffered a revolution, and France, Great Britain, and the United States experienced mutinies in the armed forces. In 1938 the attendees at the Eighteenth Party Congress in Moscow were told that in the next world war the proletariat would convert the imperialist war into a civil war. But despite the impulse to maintain neutrality in a world war, the Soviet Union only succeeded in doing so from September, 1939, to June, 1941.

Scholars hardly agree on why the Soviet Union failed. Former communists and Marxists are inclined to assign the major blame to the German Communist Party, which failed to oppose the nazis directly in 1932 and treated the German Social Democrats as the chief enemy. Although this must be accounted an error in hindsight, no matter what one's political vantage point, it seems excessive to rest the whole case for the nazi assumption of power on a short-lived tactic. Nazism's roots were too profound, too much an outgrowth of the political destructiveness of World War I, to be explained so unicausally.

Some anti-communist liberals have placed the blame for World War II (and thereby also that part of the war in which the Soviet Union participated) on the Western democracies. They argue, and quite correctly, that the Western democracies were extremely reluctant to engage in war with Hitler. This reluctance went so far that they watched passively, wringing their hands all the while, as Hitler demolished one after another of their political positions. They argue further that the Soviet Union was eager to join in collective action against nazi Germany and that if the democratic states had only tendered the invitation, nazi Germany would have been either deterred or more easily beaten. Western fastidiousness was, in this view, both the cause and the justification of the Nazi-Soviet Nonaggression Pact of 1939.

From the Soviet point of view, however, the Nazi-Soviet pact represented the optimal objective. The Soviet goal of neutrality in an imperialist war could obviously be better served by neutrality than by joining one imperialist country in war against another. It was of course psychologically more comfortable for the democratic foes of nazism to believe that all of Germany's enemies had more in common ideologically with each other than with nazism. They ignored the unambiguous Soviet analysis that fascism was only one form of capitalism.

For a time it seemed as if Stalin's policy had been crowned with success. The capitalists were destroying themselves. But why was this success so brief and illusory? With hindsight one is inclined to isolate as most critical the Soviet overestimation of French strength and resolve. Had the Soviet leaders been able to foresee, as very few did, that France would fall so quickly, they might have had more misgivings about the benefits of neutrality than they did in August, 1939. Even so, the Soviet Union could hardly have acted much differently in the summer of 1939.

Just as the Soviet Union wished to remain neutral, allowing the capitalists to destroy each other, so France and Great Britain would have preferred to remain neutral in a Russo–German war. The second desire was more difficult to effect than the first because of geographical considerations. Poland and Czechoslovakia lay between Germany and Russia; since neither would lend its territory for the passage of German armies, each had to be eliminated before a Russo–German war would become a genuine possibility. Czechoslovakia was persuaded to accept the alternative of piecemeal absorption by Germany rather than fight with her reluctant ally France. It was feared that Poland, too, might be forced into accepting German demands and not insisting that France fulfill her treaty obligations. If this could have been effected, then the fear that the Soviet Union and its friends abroad had voiced so insistently—namely, that Great Britain and France were plotting to direct Germany's armies against the Soviet Union—would have been realized. But as soon as Great

Britain committed itself to the defense of Poland (as it was not committed to the defense of Czechoslovakia), that long-feared possibility was eliminated for the Soviet Union. Furthermore, if the Poles rejected the demands that the nazis were making with increasing insistence, a German-Polish war would break out, involving both the French and the British. The conclusion of a Nazi-Soviet nonaggression pact meant that Hitler could proceed without undue concern about the two front war he had sworn to avoid, Poland not qualifying as a front. Certainly the record is clear that whatever the ineptitude of the French and the British, the latter of whom even preferred, it seemed, to fight without the Soviet Union, the Soviet Union clearly welcomed sitting out the war. As a result of the Nazi-Soviet pact the Soviet leaders probably were confirmed in their conviction that the states of the opposition camp could be played off against each other.

Although this belief, often expressed in Soviet writings and a major theme of Stalin's last official pronouncement in 1952, was probably genuine, one wonders if the Soviets believed it to their interest to play capitalist states against each other to the point of precipitating war. The Nonaggression Pact encouraged Hitler to go to war. Perhaps the Soviet leaders realized from this that large-scale war was hazardous, that evenly balanced powers might not exhaust each other, and that the victorious power might attack the Soviet Union. Since official Soviet writing has never admitted a Soviet role in the outbreak of World War II, no material is available for an analysis of Soviet attitudes toward precipitating war among other states, although Stalin expressed his keen disappointment in the wartime role of the German proletariat to Charles Bohlen at Tehran. Moreover, another opportunity to precipitate war among capitalist states never presented itself. (It does seem likely, however, that the present official Soviet concern with the danger of international tension reflects a genuine concern that wars can expand, unexpectedly, to the detriment of the Soviet Union.)

Although the Soviet Union wanted to avoid war or at least postpone its outbreak even more strongly after World War II than before, dogmatic convictions left little room for optimism. In the Soviet analysis the causes of war in the imperialist system were economic, and nothing had transpired to change the belief that capitalism would again suffer the economic depressions that produced wars. Forced industrialization and militarization therefore seemed as appropriate in the present and future as in the past, when a slower rate of industrialization and smaller armed forces would have meant Soviet defeat in World War II. The very existence of the Soviet armed forces had played an important deterrent role, since the sharp defeats administered to Japan in 1938 and 1939 had influenced the Japanese to expand southward rather than northward. Thus after World War II the Soviet leadership—and this increasingly meant Stalin alone—was confident that most of the principles upon which it had based its conduct were still valid.

The cold war can be defined in several ways. For the purposes of this account it will be defined as that state of international relations in which the world was divided into two ideological camps, in which both sides viewed the neutrality of states outside either system as transitory, and in which accretions to the strength of either side were viewed as irreversible. Each side wanted to avoid a military confrontation, but both accepted it as a possibility and accordingly prepared for it. Permanent and increasing tension was the mutual expectation. To anticipate slightly and to define the cold war in terms of the period following it, the cold war began to end when these characteristic guides to policy were altered. With the disintegration of alliance discipline in both camps, it became possible to pursue different policies toward individual countries within each system, and the concept of an ideologically divided world became less useful as a guide to state policy. Not only was the neutrality of the uncommitted states accepted, but within each system member states moved toward partial disengagement. Instead of the expectation of ever heightening tension that could destroy the world, the possibility of avoiding war and of creating areas of coincidence of interest emerged. Conflict of interests still flourished, and few leaders on either side expected a steady progression toward more amicable relations between the two superpowers. It does not seem useful to apply the term "cold war" to the new state of affairs since it differs from the old in these important aspects.

At the end of World War II, from the Soviet point of view, the tactic of playing one power against another seemed less feasible because there was now only one major adversary, the United States. All the other great powers, including those not actually occupied by the enemy, suffered great losses, from which only some have recovered. But the United States had grown marvelously in industrial strength; the American occupying forces provided the only hope its enemies had of emerging from the desolation of their ruins; America's allies were dependent on her generosity for the daily needs of existence. At this point Soviet leaders could hardly think of dividing the capitalist powers among themselves. Only mutual hostility between the Soviet Union and a capitalist camp controlled by the United States seemed possible.

Nothing had happened to alter the Soviet conviction that the basic conflict was still between capitalism and communism, and that capitalists might once again make war upon the Soviet Union. The problem, as before, was to defer that day as long as possible, hopefully until capitalism had collapsed, but more probably until the Soviet Union was in a better military position to survive a war than it was in 1945.

Like all military people, or perhaps like all people, Soviet generals could see the future only as an extension of the past, and it seemed urgently important to them to surround the Soviet Union with pliant states to allow time for the preparation of a more satisfactory defense than in June, 1941. The problem was complicated by the necessity of postponing the development of an aggressive American anti-Soviet policy.

President Roosevelt had told Stalin that he wanted to withdraw American forces from Europe within two years after the conclusion of the war. America's rapid demobilization suggested that Truman accepted that goal. Perhaps it meant that American war weariness and shortsightedness might give the Soviet Union a period of respite. For a short time Stalin permitted such views to be put forward. Eugene Varga, the most prominent Soviet economist, had argued that capitalism was in a position to stabilize itself for a time. Since in the Marxist lexicon capitalist proclivity to make war was highest when the system was wracked by crises, the prediction of stabilization was a prediction of peace. This comforting prognosis was soon denounced as incorrect: capitalism was not able to postpone its doom, it was felt, and it would consequently resort to new wars. In his speech announcing the inauguration of a first postwar Five Year Plan for industrialization Stalin made clear that the Soviet Union was to base its policy on a pessimistic expectation of the future. We will probably never know what events moved Stalin to decide that it was impossible (incorrect in his language) to expect a moderate level of cooperation to continue. He was too suspicious a man to reveal himself to even his intimates.

The cold war would probably have occurred with or without Stalin because it derived from the differing objectives of the two systems. But the difference in objectives went beyond the ordinary desire of great powers to increase their strength and influence at the expense of one another. The Soviets believed, and they so persuaded many of their opponents, that good relations could only be a phase since the two systems could not exist indefinitely side by side.

Once American leaders ceased to insist that the Soviet Union was democratically inclined because it was an ally, noncommunists, like communists, came to accept that the struggle for dominance would last for a long time. With the benefit of hindsight we now realize that the struggle was not destined to become increasingly intense and dangerous and that areas of coincidence of interest could be cleared in the larger arena of conflict of interests. It is possible to isolate particular junctures where one side wanted to abate or to break off the contest for a while and the other either did not recognize the alteration in intention or feared the consequences of a mistaken judgment on that subject. But such an exercise is meaningless. The statesmen of the late forties could not possibly have foreseen the future. They felt deeply that prudence dictated planning for a grim future.

This contest was perhaps more intense and longer in duration than it might have been because each party misperceived the intentions of the other. This complex issue deserves a few words of explanation. Perception of the long-range intentions or optimal goals of the other side was correct enough. The Soviet Union wanted to spread its control as far as possible in the areas where the collapse of German and Japanese power had created opportunities and to encourage the disintegration of capitalism. The United States, as soon as it abandoned the notion that the socialism of the Soviet Union was a way station to "democracy," wanted to thwart Soviet purposes. On this level mutual understanding was almost perfect. Misperception played its role in the development of events on the lesser but still crucial questions of judging what each side could and was willing to do at particular junctures. Was the United States willing to accept the communization of China without intervening directly or by giving support to the Chinese government? Stalin judged that the United States would not passively accept such a momentous shift in the balance of power, but he was mistaken. This mistake led to another mistake—the judgment that the United States would accept the loss of South Korea. Thus, Stalin's misconception of U.S. dispositions led to a major conflict from which neither the Soviet Union nor the United States profited.

Both sides tended to view the struggle as mortal: the communists defined the struggle between the two systems by this outcome; the United States believed that communization was an irreversible process. Few on both sides foresaw in the late 1940s that Soviet control in eastern Europe would start to recede so soon. (The significance of the Yugoslav ability to survive ejection from the communist camp was, for example, underestimated.) And even if the present degree of eastern European independence had been foreseen, it probably would not have made any difference at that time. Each decision was made on the assumption that the conflict would mount in intensity and might well result in war. Thus, even though it was realized that the opponent, at a particular juncture, might be continuing verbal pyrotechnics while preparing a tactical retreat, acting on such interpretations seemed reckless in eastern Europe and elsewhere. This was the product neither of wickedness nor of stupidity. The opponents judged each other in a policy setting, and policy's servants are not prone to take risks with the nation's vital interests.

At first the United States responded uncertainly to the ever clearer evidences of Soviet intentions to gain and retain control over parts of eastern Europe. In the initial reaction a distinction can usefully be made between the views of the professional specialists on the Soviet Union and those of the political leaders. George Kennan's contemporary papers, some of which are reproduced or summarized in his memoirs, furnish the only statement of the specialists' view. It was felt that although not much could be done to prevent the Soviet Union from consolidating political control in the areas occupied by its troops, what could not be prevented should not be sanctioned by the pretense that the will of the populations of eastern Europe could find expression in postwar political arrangements agreed upon by the United States and the Soviet Union. It was better to negotiate clearcut understandings with the Soviet Union without cant about self-determination. Stalin, it was expected, would respect such a bargain, which would make for a more manageable postwar Europe—more than in fact resulted. But these recommendations fell on deaf ears at first, not even receiving the attention of rejection.* The proponents of these views were considered to be doctrinarily anti-Soviet and therefore properly to be waved aside.

In hindsight this analysis and the recommendation implicit in it were undoubtedly right. The United States was quite unprepared to make war again so soon after a major war for any but the most compelling of reasons, and Soviet control of eastern Europe did not qualify as such. It would have been better to have accepted then what we accepted later and to have eschewed the pretense that these areas could enjoy self-determination. By accepting Soviet control in eastern Europe without approving it, we would have been in a position to request that the Soviet Union do the same in western Europe. Had such an agreement been reached after World War II (and at this remove it seems theoretically possible), one important feature of

---

* Kennan's contemporary statements of such views are the only ones for which I can find a published record. I recall two other oral expressions of such views, but the lapse of time makes it improper to repeat them or to ascribe them to individuals.

the cold war would have been absent—namely, the mutual fear that eastern or western Europe, as the case might be, was under threat requiring countermeasures.

Such a realistic approach to foreign policy was, however, more properly to be expected from a society organized on aristocratic principles than on popular ones. It might be said, parenthetically, that the realist school of foreign policy also suffered from excessive hopes for the pursuit of rational self-interest by democratic societies and in doing so committed the academic sin of confusing the normative with the analytical approach. In fact, the nature of the American system made so calculated a policy a political impossibility. The United States had entered the war and fought it with little of the enthusiasm and moral fervor of World War I. It was an unpleasant task to be rapidly dispatched so that the postponed satisfactions of normal life could be resumed. Leaders who insisted that the retention of large standing armies was a national necessity could expect little public support at the polls. To expect to drive a satisfactory bargain with the Soviet leaders while American arms were being laid down was unrealistic, and the effective decision was made not to seek a division of Europe into spheres of influence. This limitation was derived from the nature of American political life but deplored by "realpolitikers." Political leaders handled this political manifestation in various ways. It was not easy with an electorate that wanted neither to serve in the army in large numbers nor to pay heavy taxes to contain communism. One approach to the problem was to deny its existence. In this approach the Soviets were more sinned against than sinning. They felt insecure because they had been encircled by enemies. If we were nice to them, they would be nice to us. The only virtue in this amalgam of well meaning pieties and vulgar psychology was that it quickly produced its own cure. Offering opportunities to, or failing to oppose, an opponent who believes that deep ideological differences exist encourages him to behave in a way that quickly dispels the assumptions that motivated the tolerant behavior in the first place. And this is indeed what happened after a while.

A second inaccurate diagnosis was made by some political leaders who were victims of the common fallacy that one's own experience has universal applicability: they firmly believed that international politics was merely a variant of domestic politics. Their very eminence testified to their ability to understand and manipulate (domestic) politics. They did not have the naive belief that psychological reassurance in the form of unilateral concessions would bring the Soviet Union to reason. They viewed politics as an endless series of negotiations, some of which resulted in mutually satisfactory "deals." The proper mixture of promises and threats, rewards and penalties, was expected in many cases to produce a *modus vivendi* or perhaps even a series of formal agreements, since a large if unspoken coincidence of interests with the Soviet Union was assumed. Roosevelt and Byrnes were the outstanding representatives of this approach. They thought *they*, the old professionals, could work out a deal with Old Joe. They could not, of course, because Old Joe believed that coincidence of interest was ephemeral.

The kind of arrangement that Roosevelt and Byrnes wanted was worked out many years later, but only after the United States had irrefutably indicated that it would fight for western Europe, and had even fought for South Korea, and after the Soviet leadership, having acquired nuclear weapons, abandoned the idea that war was inevitable. But without these crucial changes, among others, in the international scene, the Roosevelt-Byrnes approach was essentially misinformed wishful thinking.

A third approach was that of the American right wing, which had some editorial assistance from former communists. It must be admitted—and for me it is an admission since, like many academicians, I classify myself as a liberal in politics—that the right wing in American politics understood the problem best. They were the possessors and guardians of great wealth and power. Like most in such a position, including their counterparts in the Soviet Union, they felt that they were charged with a sacred trust. Perhaps because they possessed wealth and power they had a better emotional understanding of those who wanted to deprive them of it than did the men of good will. For good reasons or bad they sensed the depth of the Soviet conviction that the struggle between the two systems was to the death. Political groups in the middle gradually adopted this stark view, but not all at once and with hesitations.

Positions were shifting, and important individuals often occupied two or more of these positions successively. The struggle between these tendencies to influence the direction of foreign policy produced an inconsistent policy. The American attitude toward the eastern European governments illustrates this condition. Although the United States accepted the force of the Soviet claim for having friendly states on its borders, the pressure from national minorities and the right wing constrained it to insist that these governments be representative—that is, democratic. But any representative Polish or Rumanian government at that point in history would have been unfriendly to the Soviet Union, especially if they received any encouragement from the United States. The Soviets, who harbored no illusions about the sentiments of the populations of eastern Europe, did not want mathematically representative governments. They demanded and got governments that represented pro-Soviet elements of political life.

Stalin interpreted the shifts of American policy toward a harder line as a demonstration of his belief that American policy was basically hostile but hoped that there might be some areas in which he could improve his position before the "hards" so dominated American policy that such efforts would be too dangerous. In probing to determine what was permitted and what was not, Stalin, of course, fed American suspicions of his intentions.

Stalin's technique of probing derived from his domestic political style. Although he discouraged factionalism in the Communist Party of the Soviet Union, he encouraged individuals to run with different balls, not revealing his preference until much later. In the rivalry of his associates Stalin saw his own security, and inscrutability was a conscious policy. For example, in 1950 Khrushchev was permitted to put forward a program for the "agrogorod" and to establish some experimental models before the idea was officially rejected. Stalin's foreign policy was conducted in the same style. Thus the Greek guerrillas were both encouraged and discouraged in their efforts to unseat the Greek government. When it seemed that their cause had foundered, Stalin could denounce the stupidity of their behavior, penalize those of his entourage who had advocated their policy, and reward the others. Thus Stalin's men were kept in constant uncertainty, not to speak of fear, and Stalin always emerged as the infallible leader. Quite obviously such a style of behavior in foreign policy frightened his opponents. Since they could not fathom what Stalin was up to, they felt it only prudent to assume that his ambitions were limitless.

But the policies adopted by the United States were clearly inadequate to oppose what were believed to be Stalin's designs. If it was believed that Stalin wanted to and could expand Soviet control toward the China Sea and the English Channel, the United States budgetary allocations to the armed forces in 1947 and 1948 were irresponsible. But the natural sponsors of the policy of containing Soviet expansion, the conservatives, suffered from two serious disabilities. First, they wished to see the Republican Party return to office after almost a generation of deprivation, and the electorate was in no mood for heroic and expensive struggles. Second, they suffered from a genuine attachment to old-fashioned economic theory. Too great a debt would ruin the nation, they believed, and they were trapped in the toils of their own dogma. Although they correctly sensed how uncompromising was Soviet hostility, they could not risk destroying the American system by having the country go bankrupt. Therefore American remobilization was neither planned nor orderly but moved forward in discrete jumps. Some in the American governmental system reluctantly agreed to what were considered necessary measures because the Soviets "were getting tougher." Others who had felt all along that the United States was complacent about communism seized upon international crises to push their case.

Five years after the war the United States had really not spent the money for the kind of military establishment that the public estimate of the threat of communism seemed to require. When it seemed as if the feeble

Greek government was about to fall to the communist guerrillas, and when the prospects for western Europe did not seem very bright either, the Democratic administration judged that they had to take some concrete steps to halt the drift of events. Since enthusiasm for new efforts in foreign policy was low, and since even the right wing was unwilling to pay for an improved military establishment, the threat of communism had to be dramatized. Although Truman's speech announcing the Truman Doctrine reread twenty years later sounds strangely restrained by comparison with later rhetoric, it was properly understood at the time as a full break with the policy of hoping for a *modus vivendi* with the Soviet Union.

It was hardly surprising that Stalin interpreted the enunciation of the Truman Doctrine and the Marshall Plan as the beginning of an American program of pressure on the Soviet Union, demonstrating the correctness of the prediction he himself had made at the end of 1946. He took the appropriate measures and largely dispensed with the fiction of multiparty regimes in eastern Europe since there was no longer any point in conciliating the Americans. (The intensity of the tightening-up process in eastern Europe probably derived as much from the shock of Tito's successful defection. This demonstrated to Stalin that a non-Soviet communist party could not be trusted to stay within the Soviet camp unless it was controlled by the Soviet police.) The savage repression of the populations of eastern Europe after 1948 confirmed the noncommunists abroad in their conviction that all communist societies were moving toward Orwell's 1984.

Heated as the rhetoric of the years 1947–49 was, it took the outbreak of the Korean War to bring the arms race to a high point from which it has never receded.

In encouraging the North Koreans to attempt to seize South Korea in a quick campaign and to present the United States with a *fait accompli*, Stalin made what turned out to be the greatest miscalculation in his postwar foreign policy. In retrospect it is easy to see why he went wrong. The events of the two previous years seemed to show that further pressure in Europe might risk a significant American response. (Moreover, the eastern European regimes were probably not considered reliable in a conflict.) But in the Far East the United States had acquiesced in the defeat of the Kuomintang with remarkable *sang froid*. It seemed as if the mainland of Asia had been written off. American passivity regarding China, combined with the desire to gain influence there, made it seem worthwhile to take a chance. Memoirs have revealed that the first steps by the United States to repel the invading forces from North Korea were much debated and the final decision taken by a very narrow margin. The American response was not foreordained; quite conceivably it might not have occurred at all. Stalin had miscalculated, but he had not taken an insane chance by any means.

Once the United States recovered from its initial defeats and crossed the 39th parallel, Stalin feared that the United States might use the opportunity to attack the Soviet Union itself with nuclear weapons. His response was to stretch his own and the eastern European economies to their limits in order to put his forces in a better state of readiness. Since he had no nuclear weapons available for his armed forces and an inadequate air-defense system, these preparations could not have deterred a United States intent on striking, nor could they have defended Soviet territory. But the expansion of his conventional forces was all Stalin could muster to deter what he conceived to be the genuine danger of an American attack.

Far from understanding that Stalin was quaking with fear, the United States too had become the prisoner of its own misjudgments and assumed that the Korean attack was a feint in preparation for a Soviet onslaught in Europe. This misconception was shared by U.S. allies in Europe, and on this foundation NATO was built. History was indeed ironical. Stalin assumed that the United States had given first priority to the defense of Europe, thus making safe the absorption of the southern half of the Korean peninsula. But the United States, convinced of the paramount importance of Europe, could only believe that Stalin was planning to attack Europe when he had the North Korean armies move southward. Consequently, not only were Stalin's wartime allies now hostile and rearmed, but West Germany too was rearmed, although without nuclear weapons. By 1948, with the defection of Yugoslavia, Europe's political-ideological boundaries were fixed. Fifteen years passed before both major parties realized this and acted accordingly.

The Korean War convinced the Soviet Union that it had reached the limits of its expansion for the time being. For the United States a formal acceptance of the status quo was out of the question because of the domestic political consequences of the Korean War. The war was unpopular in the United States and its course had nourished the political obscurantism endemic in most societies. Frustration with the heavy cost of merely restoring the status quo antebellum in Korea, and the realization of the significance of the communization of China, produced the search for scapegoats. We were unwilling to face the hard truth that China was lost because it could not have been saved, and we embarked on a disgraceful and self-damaging search for the traitors in the State Department and the Department of Defense cafeteria.

In such an atmosphere it was difficult to exploit the success of the policy of containment. Although the United States had overreacted somewhat out of an exaggerated appraisal of Stalin's willingness to take risks, it had largely followed the course recommended by George Kennan in 1947. The United States had neither attacked the Soviet Union nor tried to dislodge it from areas it had occupied, but it had convinced the Soviet leadership that further expansion was both risky and expensive. Quite clearly, after Stalin's death the Soviet Union was prepared to call something of a halt in the cold war, although the exigencies of its domestic politics somewhat obscured the expressions of that desire. Beria was willing perhaps to make radical changes in East Germany, but he was killed by his associates before his intentions could become clear to outsiders. Malenkov stated quite explicitly that the danger of a nuclear war made it necessary to end the cold war. In the heyday of McCarthyism, however, Soviet overtures could hardly be recognized and their promise assessed.

The failure to recognize, or the political inability to act upon, the first Soviet feelers for a restructuring of mutual relationships did not interfere with Dulles' plans. Believing that a *modus vivendi* was impossible, Dulles viewed any negotiations on that subject as subversive of the morale of the alliance system that contained communism. Besides being confident that communism would collapse because of its inner weakness, Dulles saw no necessity for a détente. He believed that a repetition of Korean-style attack was possible and that a country could pass over to communism from internal political decay. Any hopes he may have nourished that the United States would be prepared in such an eventuality to repeat the Korean experience were dispelled by Congress's effective veto on active military

support for the French in Vietnam in 1954.* Eisenhower made no effort to persuade Congress to change
its mind. The only weapon remaining to Dulles was
threatening the Soviet Union with American nuclear
power, which at that time was virtually a monopoly.
He extended the protection presumably created by
this threat to all noncommunist countries who asked
for it and tried to persuade those who did not ask that
they were in danger.

This policy served quite well, probably because there
was such a moderate Soviet (or for that matter Chinese) impulse to test it, but its effect was the continuation of the mutual misperception. Once the United
States enunciated the policy of massive retaliation with
nuclear weapons, it was generally assumed, both by
those who voiced the policy and by the public that
accepted it, that the Soviet Union must be on the point
of committing some great misdeed. No less a danger
seemed to justify so wholesale a threat. The Soviet
leaders could not help but worry (although they hoped
their worries were unfounded) that an uncontrolled
series of events or American malignity might cause the
execution of the threat. Sometimes, too, they seemed to
fear that the United States was seeking a pretext for a
preventive war.

---

* It is noteworthy that the then Senator Lyndon B. Johnson
played a major role in opposing the dispatch of American troops
to the Asian mainland.

IV

THE SEARCH FOR NUCLEAR COEXISTENCE: PHASE ONE TO OCTOBER, 1962—THE MOVABLE STATUS QUO

The Changed Atmosphere of Soviet Policy-Making

With the death of Stalin and conclusion of the Korean War the situation was ripe for mutual acceptance of the status quo. I have already described the inhibitions to perceiving such an opportunity and acting upon it in the United States and now turn to the political atmosphere in which Soviet aims were formulated and policies executed.

As pointed out above, Stalin in foreign as in domestic policy permitted two courses to be run simultaneously, and then as events unrolled he would enunciate the "correct" course. His successors also talked about left and right deviations and put the party imprimatur on the "correct" policy. But the similarity was only superficial. Stalin was a dictator, however that term is to be defined.

The dictatorship of his successors was one of group rule, and the political differences between the rule of one and of several were profound. Although it was not then immediately obvious, it now seems clear that the highest Soviet political organs represent a consensus of group interests. The political base of the most powerful leader or leaders is in constant motion, and no regular procedure exists to determine which interest or, more correctly, congeries of interests is to prevail on particular issues. Hence any leadership can be retired if it cannot command an unknown fraction of the political base at a particular juncture. The extent and the form of that support is not readily predictable for two reasons.

First, it is not clear to what body or bodies the Soviet leadership answers. Is it the Politburo (or Presidium)? What is the role of the Secretariat? When is there recourse to the whole Central Committee of the Communist Party? The best that can be said is that these factors vary with the situation.

Second, no majority principle governs procedure in whatever body constitutes the political judge of the top leadership. The Soviet Union, itself the successor to a government based on a hierarchical society, is constructed on strict hierarchical principles in which the motto "one man-one vote" is meaningless. There is a truth, a correct line, which only the Communist Party is fit to discover and promulgate. Within the party not all are equally fitted. The terminology of modern Western political theory is inadequate to describe how a decision is reached in the Soviet Union. One must have recourse to the language of an earlier age of hierarchy and established truth. In a medieval cathedral chapter it was not the majority but the *maior et sanior pars* that made a decision—quality as well as numbers were taken into account.

The uncertainty about who decides and how the votes are weighed affects both the perception of the outside world and the course of action adopted in response to those perceptions. Foreign and domestic policies in the Soviet Union as elsewhere are interrelated, that is to say, they come in clusters. Only academics can evaluate issues one at a time; the political actor must pick them up in bunches. Thus the military budget and the allocations for heavy industry are related to a perception of the requirements that the international situation may place upon the defense establishment. This in turn affects the resources available to the consumer sector. Therefore a Soviet pronouncement that international tension is increasing or decreasing, that capitalism is in a period of stabilization or in a period of crisis, has direct implications for various political interests. At times such formulas are uttered out of a genuine conviction that the international situation has changed; at other times "estimates" are deliberately manipulated to support a particular line in domestic policy. Once an assessment is made, efforts are made to demonstrate its validity. Thus in 1959 part of Khrushchev's support derived from those who aspired to satisfy Soviet consumer needs and believed that a relaxation of international tension was necessary for that purpose. In this political setting it was to Khrushchev's advantage to insist that Eisenhower was a man of peace and to meet him personally and publicly. Khrushchev's opponents, who felt for one reason or another that relaxation at home and abroad was a mistaken or premature policy, sought to prove that the United States was bellicose rather than pacific. At times these opponents exercised their internal political power, especially with the security police, to create incidents demonstrating that international tension was increasing. Into the line of sight along which international reality was viewed were inserted two distorting lenses: those of ideology and partisan politics. The pronouncements emitted by this system had a certain arcane quality. Those who sought to penetrate their meaning were described with the not altogether flattering epithet of Kremlinologists. This interpretative effort was only partially satisfactory, precisely because the key questions of relations with the capitalist world, relations with major allies, and their implications for domestic policy were unresolved in the Soviet Union. Thus only rarely could Kremlinologists maintain that a particular Soviet policy had been adopted and would be consistently pursued for a long time. More often they had to say that a Soviet policy was in flux and that different resolutions were possible. The necessary indeterminancy of the analysis permitted a continued belief that Soviet policy was an enigma and that the only safe course was to assume that the Soviet Union was indiscriminately malign and aggressive. I am not suggesting that inside the crusty Soviet exterior a handsome prince of peace was struggling to emerge and that if only the United States had understood that truth and pronounced the magic words, he would have been freed of his bonds. Soviet statements and behavior admitted of many interpretations because they reflected the internal political struggle to appraise the possibilities and the methods of coexistence with the capitalist world. Even the advocates of coexistence in the Soviet Union argued for a settlement with the United States on the basis of a "rolling" or "movable" status quo,* and what that might have been was not easy for the other party to the status quo to divine.

The Shifting Military Status Quo

The Soviet attitude toward relations with capitalist countries changed significantly as the implications of nuclear weapons were assimilated. The new approach found expression in many forms, but the most familiar are probably the most significant. The thesis presented at the Twentieth Congress of the Communist Party that war was not necessarily inevitable and the increased

---

* I am indebted to Vernon V. Aspaturian for this idea.

emphasis on the peaceful path to socialism reflected two Soviet realizations. One, that the Soviet Union could not recover from the disaster of a nuclear war and, two, that the strongest capitalist power had made, or was making, a similar assessment. If this analysis was correct, and one can readily understand the powerful impulse to seize it, coexistence would have to be differently defined. It was no longer merely an interlude of the relaxation of conflict during which the Soviet Union could build its economic-military strength. Now the greatest socialist power and the greatest capitalist power had a common interest that stretched into the indefinite future. It meant that the sruggle between the capitalist and communist worlds was limited by a common desire to survive. Coexistence was no longer merely expediential and temporary.

The awful prospect of mankind destroying itself in a nuclear Armageddon gripped the imagination of the entire world, a world to which the Soviet Union increasingly felt related. Earlier Soviet leaders, because they were weaker than their opponents and expected to become stronger, wanted to avoid war as long as possible. Now that they wanted to avoid nuclear war and since they very much feared that any direct engagement with the United States could lead to such a war, they felt it necessary to avoid any war with the United States indefinitely.

With the acceptance of such an aim and the judgment that its accomplishment was possible, the traditional Soviet view of the future had to be modified. War could no longer be welcomed as the midwife of revolution; capitalists, it now had to be assumed, feared war so much that capitalism now could sink into desuetude and leave the stage of history without the final spasm of war so long predicted and feared by the communists. Such a changed view of the more distant future had implications for short-run policies. It was now necessary to achieve some relaxation of tension in relations with the United States. But the Soviet Union wanted to improve its military, economic, and political position before accepting a more or less permanent balance.

In 1954 Malenkov and others warned that a new world war would doom all civilization. Khrushchev, when he replaced Malenkov in 1955, gained some crucial domestic support by denying the validity of this analysis. But as Khrushchev consolidated his political position and felt he could dispense with the political support of those to whom Malenkov's views were either anathema or politically inconvenient, he increasingly adopted Malenkov's position and made it his political motto.

In the years 1954–55 the gap between Soviet and U.S. military power was probably wider than it had ever been before or would be again. The two great military-industrial establishments were moving in different rhythms. They both expanded greatly during the Korean War, but an important fraction of the American expansion was in nuclear weapons and strategic-delivery systems. At the end of the Korean War and even more so in 1954–55, the United States was able to do what Dulles warned it might do. His was no empty threat. In those years the United States on very short notice could have destroyed as much of the Soviet industry and population as it willed, secure in the belief that the Soviet retaliation against the United States would have been trifling.

From the Soviet point of view this was hardly the time to reach a *modus vivendi* with the United States based on the status quo. Even estimating their prospects conservatively, the Soviet leaders could be confident that the then unfavorable balance of power was transitory and that in a very short time they would be narrowing the gap in military strength. As early as 1954 Khrushchev remarked in an unguarded moment that Dulles' policy of moving from a position of strength was not a bad thing and that the Soviets hoped to do the same soon.* The military balance was of course the most dramatic aspect of national power, but the Soviet leaders expected that their economic position would improve rapidly, too. The communist ideology enjoins optimism about the future, and in this regard Khrushchev was the best of communists. Besides, the idea of a bipolar world was advanced as a truism by scholars and statesmen. No one really dissented from the prediction that the Soviet Union would become relatively and absolutely more powerful. Uncertainty centered on how much the balance would shift. In the Soviet Union both those who wanted to come to a settlement and those who believed it was not possible agreed that the existing situation had to be altered, particularly in the military sphere.

Although Western commentators talked loosely about coming nuclear parity, the Soviets knew they had far to go to achieve that goal. The great disparity in military strength made it inadvisable to negotiate any arms freeze or leveling off, if only because at any point until 1962 (the period we are now examining) clear Soviet inferiority would have become obvious to all. Hence Soviet aims were best served by creating an atmosphere in which the United States would not press ahead too rapidly, while the Soviet Union could improve her relative position.

---

* Khrushchev's unguarded moments were not infrequent, much to the discomfiture of his associates and the benefit of the analyst.

It was much easier to formulate such a program than to effectuate it for several reasons. First, not all in the Soviet Union believed that a rough settlement with the United States was possible, and instead of arming to parley, they believed in arming to deter, to force concessions, or to wage war if necessary. Accepting the possibility of war as the basis for planning, as professional military leaders must, nothing less than equality was a prudent goal. For others, the pursuit of military equality bore the price tag of slowing the Soviet economic progress that they considered essential for the creation of a bipolar power system. Second, American perception of growing Soviet military power might stimulate greater American efforts that would leave the Soviets considerably poorer and no stronger relatively. (Indeed this is what happened.) Khrushchev was therefore under great pressure to demonstrate that there was no genuine danger of war from the United States and that an inferior military position was an adequate platform for Soviet political advance. Political gains would be the best weapon against those in the Soviet Union who despised Khrushchev as complacent. The political problem for Khrushchev was to convince domestic opposition that the Soviet Union was about to make, or was already making, important political advances (to which, of course, he himself had no intrinsic objection) while at the same time he had to convince his foreign opposition that he was making only minor adjustments in the status quo. Adroit and skillful as he was, this task was beyond Khrushchev's powers.

In the United States these initial years of post-Stalinist coexistence presented a quite different aspect. After the Korean War those who had once hoped that the Soviet Union could be induced to adopt a more temporate course by a program of reassuring political therapy were not ready to revive that blighted hope; those on the right wing of American politics who felt that the Soviet menace had been minimized and the counter-measures inadequate were resolved not to permit a return to the slackness of years before the Korean War. All agreed—some resignedly, some belligerently—that the Soviet Union represented a genuine threat to American security. The problem was how much and what kind of preparation to make to deal with the problem.

The Eisenhower administration represented a peculiar amalgam of ambitions and inhibitions which in combination permitted the maintenance of Soviet hopes in some version of coexistence. To be somewhat unkind, but perhaps not unfair, it had a big stick, a big mouth, a tight hand on the pursestrings, and a commitment to inaction. We shall presently examine how this compound affected the resolution of the outstanding political problems with the Soviet Union. In the military sphere its parsimony was a critical factor. In his pronouncements as well as his appointments Eisenhower exhibited an attachment to extremely conservative economic principles. He believed that the fabric of the national life could be torn asunder by the assumption of too great a debt, and he took his duty as steward of his country's substance just as seriously as his task as the guardian of her gates. He, too, contemplated the prospect of nuclear war with horror but also believed that capitalism and communism had competing goals. He tried therefore to conduct relations with the Soviet Union in an amicable atmosphere, without yielding any positions, and with the minimum expenditure prudence permitted.

The Soviet plans for their military establishment were difficult to penetrate. They were undoubtedly trying to reduce the distance between the Soviet Union and the United States, but were they really aiming to outstrip the United States and then press from a position of superior strength? To answer the question satisfactorily one would have to read the Soviet mind, or to be more accurate, the Soviet minds that contended on this issue. The American military establishment in the past had without exception received less than they requested and sometimes critically less than they had needed. They had become habituated to ask for more than they expected to get and to put their case in the form of estimates of the putative enemy's capacities. Usually they resolved the ambiguities inherent in intelligence data in favor of the higher estimates. Eisenhower had spent much of his career in this atmosphere and felt quite secure in paring requests to what he conceived to be budgetary realities. But like most who have risen to the top of the American military hierarchy, he was neither doctrinaire nor unaccustomed to yield strongly held views when subjected to political pressure. Hence when the Soviet Union developed and demonstrated the first artificial earth satellite, the sputnik, Eisenhower permitted the inauguration of an expensive and very successful program to develop and procure American intercontinental missiles.*

The U–2 Incident

The Soviet Union was surprised at the rapidity of the American acquisition of ICBM's, perhaps the most politically potent of modern weapons. When this striking American success was contrasted with Khrushchev's

*A very modestly financed effort to produce an American artificial earth satellite had been underway for some years before.

failure to make political gains on the basis of Soviet nuclear power, it called into question the wisdom of his whole political-military strategy. The U-2 incident played a crucial role in the Soviet reappraisal. Some of the generalizations about coexistence that I have made for the period before 1962 can be illustrated by recalling some of the main features of this incident.

The U-2 reconnaissance planes had been taking photographs for several years before one of its pilots survived the destruction of his aircraft on May 1, 1960. The American possession of numerous photographs of the Soviet Union explains why Eisenhower had been so confident that the American military forces were adequate. One is tempted to speculate that these flights may have served another function in the relations between the Soviet Union and the United States. To the Soviets it provided the reassurance that Eisenhower was pursuing his moderate policy toward the Soviet Union, to be described shortly, in full knowledge of the great disparity between Soviet and American forces. Had Eisenhower's moderation been based on overestimates of Soviet strength, it might have been abandoned when he became undeceived. Since Eisenhower made no strong statements about Soviet inferiority during the domestic controversy about the missile gap, the Soviets could conclude that he was sufficiently interested in some sort of *modus vivendi* to eschew the political advantages he might have gained from publicly insisting on Soviet weakness. Whether he was fully conscious of it or not, Eisenhower had acted as Khrushchev's political ally in the Soviet domestic struggle. By receiving him at Camp David as an equal (no other Soviet or Russian leader had been so received in the United States) Eisenhower supported Khrushchev's argument in the Soviet internal political controversy that Soviet military strength was adequate for Soviet political purposes. How could one argue convincingly that the Soviet Union was despised and abused because of its military weakness when Khrushchev had been received with such respect in the United States?

When the U-2 was downed, Khrushchev yielded to the temptation to make some immediate political gains. This was to be a costly error but was perhaps unavoidable, since from Khrushchev's point of view his internal political position required bolstering by some victory, while Eisenhower's did not.

Khrushchev's first response was roughly joshing and calculated to embarrass Eisenhower. Khrushchev boasted about the performance of his surface-to-air missiles (SAM's) but concealed the pilot's survival in order to elicit an American explanation that could be demolished by producing the pilot. When the U.S. authorities fell into the trap, Khrushchev crowed over Eisenhower's discomfiture and confidently demanded an apology or a repudiation of presidential responsibility. Here he failed to consider Eisenhower's domestic political situation. Although Eisenhower was generally disdainful of criticism, he was stung by remarks that he spent too much time on the golf course and that, in effect, he was a figurehead who reigned while others ruled. It was politically impossible and probably personally repugnant for him to apologize by explaining that the flights had taken place without his knowledge. Eisenhower stated instead that the United States had the *right* to keep the Soviet Union under surveillance because U.S. security demanded it. Although not so intended, this was taken as a terrible insult. Great powers, friendly and unfriendly, satisfy their curiosity about each other's affairs clandestinely, but, if caught, usage dictates either bald denial or charging a subordinate with exceeding his authority. To insist that one has the right to spy on another power is to add insult to intrusion.

Khrushchev's only recourse was to fume, rant, and try to divide the United States from her allies, but to no avail. He had to abandon his effort to roll the status quo back a bit in Berlin and to satisfy himself with the announcement that he would wait until a new president was in office. This setback weakened Khrushchev's domestic position, and he was never able to effect the proposal he had enunciated in January, 1960, for a major reduction of the Soviet military establishment. The U-2 affair demonstrated how internal political necessities in both countries made even negotiation of outstanding issues difficult. No one can now say if some agreement on Berlin in the spring of 1960 could have been reached.

The Intensification of the Arms Race under Kennedy's Administration

With President Kennedy a new era opened in Soviet-American relations. During his brief term of office mutual misperception and misunderstanding were supplanted by a short but significant period of improved mutual appreciation of the coincidence of interest. Let us examine this briefly in the military sphere before turning to the politics.

Where the Eisenhower administration tended to be complacent if not torpid, the Kennedy administration was ambitious and activist. The Eisenhower administration was suspicious of intellectuals; Kennedy recruited them. Eisenhower was a fiscal conservative;

Kennedy was converted to Keynesianism. The style of the new administration very much influenced the nature of the relations between the two great powers. The Eisenhower administration had never made out a very rigorous intellectual case for its military program; it was content to claim that General Eisenhower knew best. Kennedy had made the missile gap a campaign issue and he appointed an energetic Secretary of Defense who was determined to be systematic, rigorous, and calculated in his military planning, rather than haphazard as his predecessors were judged to have been.

In the judgment of the new directors of foreign and military policy massive retaliation was bankrupt. If the Soviet Union should repeat the pounce-and-snatch technique in Berlin that had almost succeeded in Korea, the United States would now have no alternatives to "holocaust or humiliation," since, unlike 1950, the Soviet Union now had nuclear weapons that could devastate Europe if not the United States. Conventional forces had to be increased in Europe. The United States hoped its new ability to respond with conventional arms would permit the Soviet Union to withdraw its challenge to a U.S. position. In addition the United States had to be prepared to deal with guerrilla warfare in noncommunist countries. (Insurgency was the term used, perhaps because guerrilla had a heroic ring.)

Since the Kennedy administration was nothing if not energetic and efficient, the U.S. military capability expanded quickly in many respects. Intercontinental ballistic missiles began to be deployed, as it turned out, earlier and in greater numbers than in the Soviet Union. The capacity to deploy ground forces quickly far from the United States was significantly increased. (Incidentally, this made possible simultaneous intervention

in Vietnam and in the Dominican Republic in early
1965.) From the Soviet point of view the acquisition of
this capability was hardly reassuring, and there is evidence that they foresaw its employment. The argu-
ments of those who charged Khrushchev with neglect-
ing Soviet military security were thus strengthened.

From the Soviet point of view the increase in ground-
force strength in Europe was not a new instrument
designed to save the world from nuclear war through
miscalculation; it was rather a demonstration that the
United States was unwilling to accept any change in
the status quo in Berlin. From the Soviet point of view
the American argument that preparation for controlled
nuclear war would avoid its worst consequences if
mutual deterrence failed was interpreted to mean, at
the most, that the United States was trying to make
nuclear war acceptable and, at the least, that the new
theory of controlled nuclear warfare was a justification
for American improvements in strategic forces. (The
second of these two interpretations was indeed correct.) The shift of the military balance in American
favor was unwelcome in the Soviet Union. From their
point of view the earlier balance had adequately maintained the American political position, which the Soviet
Union had never dared challenge directly since the
Korean War. Could it be that Kennedy was attempt-
ing some new pressure on the Soviet Union?

Those in the Soviet Union committed to the possibility of détente seemed to have concluded that the
United States was trying to alter the military balance
in its favor before reaching a settlement, formal or in-
formal, part of which would presumably be an agreement to keep military forces at the existing levels.
Their opponents, who rejected the possibility of such
a settlement, suspected that the United States was seek-

ing to improve its military position in order to put pressure upon the Soviet Union or its allies. They were able to stifle whatever impulse existed to conclude a formal agreement on nuclear testing and to end the unofficial moratorium on nuclear testing in the fall of 1961. The Soviet announcement of the resumption of nuclear testing and the development of nuclear bombs of greater power and antimissile defenses followed hard upon official American statements, most notably that of Undersecretary of Defense Roswell Gilpatric, that the United States was greatly superior to the Soviet Union in nuclear capacities.*

This was a significant departure from the practice of the Eisenhower administration. Eisenhower had made general statements that a missile gap did not exist, thus making it possible for the Soviet Union to claim superiority in very general terms. The Kennedy administration statements were specific, and their insistent tone suggested that if necessary more evidence could be furnished. This of course strengthened the position of anti-Khrushchevites in the Soviet Union. The Soviet military establishment, they argued, needed more not less support.

In such an atmosphere it was very difficult to expect that the Soviet leaders would have accepted any wide-ranging measures of inspection. Soviet secrecy has almost always been employed to conceal weakness not strength. As a matter of fact they have been quick to boast about strength and have on occasion tried to mislead the United States in this way. The presence of

---

* "The destructive power which the United States could bring to bear, even after a Soviet surprise attack upon our forces, would be as great as, perhaps greater than, the total undamaged force which the enemy can threaten to launch against the United States in a first strike." *The New York Times,* October 22, 1961.

international inspection agencies in the Soviet Union at a time when the United States insisted on great superiority could only be viewed as another instrument to demonstrate Soviet weakness. Although there is little doubt that both Kennedy and Khrushchev were genuinely interested in some sort of a test ban agreement in 1961, they both acted or felt forced to act in ways that made that impossible.

The Kennedy administration's specialists suffered from the doctrinaire rigidity peculiar to those who have to defend policies they have recommended. Convinced that an increase in American military power was necessary, and arguing that it was of mutual benefit, they were incapable, or unwilling, to imagine that the Soviet leadership might have a different view of the situation. They felt that the logic of their position was so compelling that in time the Soviets would come to accept it. At the end of his first year in office Kennedy stated in an interview in *The New York Times* of January 16, 1962 that his greatest disappointment was the failure to secure a nuclear test ban treaty. He was a victim of restricted vision. Since he knew that he was intensely desirous of a test ban agreement, he could not understand that to the Soviet leadership his actions in the military sphere seemed to belie that aim.

For their part the Soviet leaders could not realize that actions that they had initiated or sanctioned caused many of Kennedy's military preparations to seem politically if not militarily necessary. After the Bay of Pigs invasion the Soviet leadership thought it safe to take Castro under their official protection, encouraging him to hope that he could extend his revolution. What better justification could preparations for counterinsurgency have had? And the resumption of Soviet pressure on Berlin seemed to justify the wisdom of the American program for the creation of stronger ground forces in Europe.

By the end of the first year of the Kennedy administration a heavier fog of misperception had settled over Soviet-American relations than had existed earlier. There was more talk of arms-control agreements, but the U.S. military budget had been increased.

The issue of military parity could be suppressed as long as the United States did not insist on its superiority. During the early part of 1962 Khrushchev was on the defensive internally because it was now demonstrated that his attempt to mislead or deceive the United States about the strategic balance had failed. Although Khrushchev now insists, and Soviet commentaries are in agreement, that the major motive in the emplacement of missiles in Cuba was the deterrence of a supposed American invasion of Cuba, the fact remains that the success of the project would have altered the strategic balance significantly. Although the United States had started from behind in the ballistic missile race, it had concentrated effort on long-range missiles and had overtaken the Soviet Union in intercontinental ballistic missiles. The Soviet Union, unlike the United States, had progressed from short-range to long-range missiles in an orderly program and had great numbers of medium-range missiles which could have reached large parts of the United States from Cuba. Since in the strategic dialogue of the time the calculus was megatons on target, Soviet medium-range missiles in Cuba were the equivalent of American intercontinental missiles in the United States. Very probably the Soviet Union reckoned that if they could initially emplace a few dozen missiles without opposition, they could later put in more.

The Soviet Union tried to alter the balance so that

both parties would be militarily less unequal. In the period after October, 1962, negotiations were undertaken in which the tacit assumption was one of non-parity of military power. This represented a significant change in the nature of the problems of coexistence.

The Shifting Political Balance

As a matter of historical fact the North Korean attack on South Korea was the last occasion when a communist state directly attacked a noncommunist state with the purpose of increasing the number of the former and decreasing the number of the latter. As indicated earlier, the opponents of the Soviet Union were slow to realize how reluctant the Soviet Union was to repeat a similar gamble elsewhere. Each party felt that the other might seek to remove an area from his own sphere, and each feared that the loss of even an area of lesser importance would demoralize others and cause the system to unravel. Even a tacit understanding on accepting the status quo could not be concluded until each side relinquished the hope, or the requirement, that the status quo must be changed somewhat before it became the basis of an agreement. For the Soviet Union the primary area of concern was eastern Europe.

Many Americans viewed the 1952 campaign rhetoric about a roll back in eastern Europe as bombast, but the Soviet leadership had to ponder whether a genuine threat lay underneath the words. The failure of the United States to intervene in the Hungarian revolution at the end of 1956 probably reassured the Soviet leadership. The Soviet Union hesitated before dispatching Soviet armies to suppress the Hungarian rebellion, but by the time the decision was taken, Secretary Dulles had indicated that the United States would not inter-

vene.* The United States was, of course, distracted by
the simultaneous crisis over the Anglo-French-Israeli
attack on the Suez Canal, but its failure to offer the
Hungarian rebels little but ambiguous verbal encouragement before the revolution, and none after it was
underway, was correctly interpreted to mean communist power in eastern Europe was not to be subject to
direct American intervention. This conviction was reinforced by U.S. passivity during the East German up-
rising in 1953, when there had been no distraction like
that of Suez. American abstention took the heart out of
whatever impulse existed in eastern Europe to revolt
against Soviet-controlled communist parties, and opposition to the Soviet Union came increasingly to be expressed through the agency of these parties. In a sense,
once the likelihood of direct American support to eastern European nationalism was discounted, the Soviet
Union could accept the manifestations of that nationalism—although it hardly encouraged them. This inaction on Eisenhower's part was perhaps his most significant contribution to the Soviet belief in the possibility
of coexistence.

The most important issue was that of Berlin and the
future of Germany. Each side feared that failure to
support its client would lead to severe political deterioration in its part of Germany. The West German state
had made a remarkable economic recovery. It was well
on the road to becoming the strongest military power in
western Europe, but it was still a client state politically.

---

* Dulles said in *The New York Times,* October 27, 1956, that
the United States had always stimulated political independence
and human liberty and that the "captive peoples should never
have reason to doubt that they have in us a sincere and dedi-
cated friend who shares their aspirations." At this crucial point,
before Soviet military intervention, Dulles did not go beyond
these vague and pious generalities.

Any intimation that the United States might reduce its support of West Germany sent perturbations through its whole body politic. This made even talk about negotiations with the Soviet Union politically upsetting to West German politicians.

The Soviet Union faced similar problems in its sector of Germany. Since the regime was unpopular and economic opportunities in West Germany were so much greater millions of East Germans fled. The majority who left were young, energetic, and trained at East German expense. Their flight represented a flow of precious capital from the poorer to the richer part of Germany. Making life in East Germany economically and politically more attractive would have alleviated the problem, but a program to do so could not be started until the hemorrhage was staunched. The first effort centered around the status of Berlin. If Berlin could be removed in one way or another from allied control, refugees would have to leave across the zonal borders, by sea, or through countries bordering on East Germany, all of which were socialist countries. If this could be accomplished, the number of refugees would be reduced to a tiny fraction and the problem would be made manageable.

At this neuralgic point in Europe the distinction between defense and offense lost its significance. One could argue that East Germany and the Soviet Union needed to stop the exodus desperately and that any action for that purpose was defensive. But one could also argue that any change in the status of West Berlin would have been interpreted in West Germany as the first in a series of U.S. concessions and that the political consequences for West Germany and NATO would have been very serious. The acceptance of the Soviet demand, whatever its motivation, would have dealt a severe blow to Western Germany, and, therefore, the United States was bound to deal with it as a Soviet and East German offensive. For the Soviet Union to accept the status quo meant acquiescence in at least the economic collapse of Eastern Germany. In the end only by giving up its claim to West Berlin and sealing off the Eastern zone could the communists stop the exodus. To maintain the economic situation in East Germany, they had to give up a political claim on West Berlin.

Earlier, however, the communists had entertained higher hopes, growing out of Khrushchev's misunderstanding of Eisenhower. The American and the Soviet modes of negotiations contributed to the confusion. The American political style of negotiating differences is for each party to assert mutuality of interest, understanding of the other party's point of view, and readiness to make some concession to it. In American terms this is an overture to negotiations, not the yielding of a major position. The negotiation takes place after each side has indicated that it is willing to yield some points without specifying which ones. Thus, when Eisenhower said that the situation was "abnormal" in Berlin he meant to convey that he was willing to negotiate about Berlin. He hardly meant that he had agreed in advance to make specific concessions.

The Soviet style of negotiation is different. They insist that the situation is very dangerous, that their maximum demands are the only basis of negotiation, and they tend not to indicate willingness to make any concessions until the end of the negotiating process. Therefore Eisenhower's statement about the abnormality of the situation was interpreted as a concession rather than as merely a signal indication of willingness to negotiate. Khrushchev, being under heavy internal political pressure, was predisposed to mislead himself and his colleagues about the significance of a single word pronounced by Eisenhower.

From this came the bitterness and sense of betrayal voiced by Khrushchev after the U-2 incident. Khrushchev had thought he was dealing with a simpleton and Eisenhower had turned out to be a wily deceiver. He was neither one nor the other, but Khrushchev could only have hoped for success if Eisenhower had been a fool and could only explain his own failure by asserting Eisenhower's perfidy. In point of fact he accused him of both.

During the Kennedy administration, however, a *de facto* agreement was arrived at, but only after two severe crises. As he had promised the East Germans, Khrushchev returned to the Berlin issue after Kennedy's election only to find very soon that Kennedy was improving his military position in Europe. The dominant American expectation was that the Soviet Union would employ a variant of the pounce-and-snatch technique of the North Korean attack on South Korea. The United States might be confronted by a *fait accompli* in West Berlin and then have to face the difficult choice of accepting it or initiating hostilities in an area where the Soviet Union had superiority. The Kennedy administration was anxious because it did not know that the Soviet leadership was unwilling to run such risks.

The administration could have spared itself its concern because its obduracy had already borne fruit. The Soviet leadership calculated that they could not get an American agreement to put West Berlin under their effective control, and the only way they saw to stop the flow of refugees was to build a barrier between West and East Berlin. The building of the wall marked the beginning of the end of the Soviet pressure on West Berlin. It meant that they were ready to accept the status quo in Berlin, and after the missile crisis to all intents and purposes the Soviet Union dropped the issue. For a while Kennedy feared that the wall represented the beginning of a new assault, but in time he realized that the Soviet Union had retreated.

Until the bombing of North Vietnam in the early part of 1965 a tacit agreement existed between the Soviet Union and the United States that neither would carry out a direct military attack on a state within the other's system. This agreement did not extend, however, to an understanding not to support revolutionary or subversive movements in the other's sphere. Even less agreement was reached on the rules of engagement in the competition for the third world.

Tension mounted rapidly in this area because of the belief, common to both contenders, that the future balance of power would be significantly affected by the outcome there. Western experience suggested that communization was an irreversible phenomenon since the dictatorship of the communist party could prevent change. In the Soviet Union the third world was seen as an area that imperialism had held in thrall for more than a century and that would progress more rapidly toward genuine independence and ultimately to socialism if the help and advice of the socialist world were available. The first step was to encourage the elimination of Western influence, and this brought the two camps into a direct conflict over issues and areas both considered of deep symbolic and actual importance.

These regions, however, were only as important as the areas that formed an integral part of each system if one made projections about their future importance. Conflict was greater over these areas because of the fluidity of the situation. The very abatement of the intensity of the cold war had introduced new uncertainties. As the cold war abated the cohesion of each system suffered. As it became evident that the United States would not, (from its own point of view) or could not any longer (from the Soviet point of view) directly intervene in the socialist countries, a precondition for the disintegration of the communist alliance had been created. As long as the possibility of an American attack had to be reckoned with, differences within the communist camp tended to be suppressed. For the secondary communist powers reasonably good relations with the Soviet Union were a necessity as long as an American attack was believed to be a genuine possibility. But as that danger seemed to recede, the centrifugal forces in the communist system found expression, so that the Soviet Union lost a good deal of whatever control it had exercised over secondary powers and lost all control over Albania and China.

The United States realized only slowly that it was not dealing with a united communist world. At the very moment that the Kennedy administration assumed office the conflict between the Soviet Union and China was approaching what turned out to be one of a series of crescendos. In the last meeting of all the communist parties in Moscow at the end of 1960 a common statement had finally been worked out in which the Communist Party of the Soviet Union agreed to formulas on the necessity for the employment of violence in the third world which went beyond what they would have preferred. On January 6, 1961, Khrushchev returned to the subject in a lengthy speech in which he retreated from the common Sino-Soviet position by reducing support of wars of national liberation. But for the new administration the speech conveyed a message opposite to what Khrushchev had intended. This was the first major Soviet pronouncement analyzed by Ken-

nedy and his advisers as officers charged with responsibility for American security. If some of the permanent
specialists in the administration realized that the January 6th speech represented a more moderate position
(as they probably did), they were either unable or unwilling to gain acceptance of that view. The new administration felt that the Cuban question ranked with
the Berlin question in seriousness and feared that Cuba
might be only the first in a series of insurgencies with
which the defense establishment was so ill-equipped to
cope. Kennedy had been determined to improve the
"conventional" forces before coming to office, and the
natural tendency was to look for support of the wisdom
of that decision in new evidence as it appeared. Even if
some administration personnel realized that Khrushchev's January 6th speech represented a retreat, they
could question his sincerity, or argue convincingly that
whatever Khrushchev had meant, one successful communist revolution would cause him to change his position.

The Kennedy administration launched with great
fanfare a program of preparing for counterinsurgency
on the assumption that guerrilla warfare when conducted by communists represented a new phenomenon
with which ratiocination and energy could deal. All
this well-advertised activity, combined with the growth
of the U.S. ground forces, unnerved the Soviet leaders,
who feared that the United States was preparing to
become the "gendarme of the world" and to support
the status quo everywhere in the belief that changes
would, or could, lead to the creation of communist
states.

Gradually it was realized that the Soviet Union was
not the undisputed master of the communist world and
that it had little control over other communist coun-

tries and even less over some communist parties. Hence it was pointless to charge the Soviet Union with responsibility for a revolutionary movement whose course it could not influence and whose inception it might have opposed. Just before his death Kennedy had relaxed his preoccupation with the dangers of changes in the status quo and seemed to accept the fact that third world countries could go their own way without American interference or pressure as long as they did not insist on calling themselves communist. In his speeches in 1963 Kennedy expressed this relaxed attitude by referring to "a world safe for diversity." Although the conflict in the third world was beginning to abate in intensity at the end of Kennedy's term in office, it was soon to revive in a new form. This revival was connected with the consequences of the Cuban missile crisis, which marked the end of the myth of duopoly.

THE SEARCH FOR NUCLEAR COEXISTENCE: PHASE TWO— AFTER THE MISSILE CRISIS

V

Kennedy and Khrushchev continued to jockey for relative advantage, believing that their countries controlled or shortly would control the politics of the world. Europe was excluded from this contest, but for a time the Soviet Union hoped that other areas, even those formally in alliance with the United States, could be detached. In this arena Khrushchev made his major misjudgment of Kennedy.

When Kennedy reluctantly agreed to activate the plan for the overthrow of Castro, he believed that a small action would energize a successful "democratic" revolution against Castro. As soon as Kennedy realized that his expectations were unfounded he cut his losses. He was unwilling to use American troops as the main agency for forcing a political change in Cuba. But as events were soon to prove, Kennedy did not hesitate to engage the whole of American military power in the contest when the issue was the balance of power between the Soviet Union and the United States. Khrushchev failed to understand that when the stakes were small Kennedy could disengage without any pressure from the Soviet Union, but that when the stakes were large Kennedy was even willing to risk war with the Soviet Union.

The missile crisis exposed the heart of the issue: would the United States permit the Soviet Union to reach rough military parity with itself? The emplacement of Soviet missiles in Cuba would not have made Castro more of a communist than he already was. But the establishment of a Soviet military base in Cuba and its equipment with medium- and intermediate-range ballistic missiles would have put the Soviet Union within easy reach of parity or superiority in the contest for capacity to destroy the opponent. If to this was added the generally accepted superiority of the Soviet theater forces in Europe, a dramatic shift in the military balance of power would have occurred. This Kennedy refused to countenance.

Once this short-cut to Soviet military parity had been barred, only the very expensive course of outbuilding the United States remained. Although the details are not clear, the issue was apparently the subject of bitter controversy in the Soviet Union. To accelerate the arms race with an opponent who had much greater industrial and economic resources might well be self-defeating. The Soviet Union had to face the prospect that its relative position might deteriorate after it had expended scarce resources on military hardware. The Soviet press carried only fragments of the counterargument and it therefore cannot be reconstructed with any confidence. Presumably the proponents of continuing the contest for military parity pointed to technological developments in defense which might give the Soviet Union qualitative superiority and recommended shifting the competition to that ground. From the pattern of Soviet weapons developments since that time it seems that the "conservative" party was able to retain some important options. First, a gradual but steady increase in the number of offensive intercontinental missiles was inaugurated and, second, research and development on ballistic missile defense was continued. Soviet decisions involving sizable resource allocations are under a constant review. By keeping the expansion of the offensive forces underway at even a moderate pace and perfecting the new defensive systems to a point where purchase and deployment could be justified, the option of ascending a new rung in the spiral of arms competition was left open. Five years later, it seems that the accumulated effect of a series of decisions has resulted in the exercise of that option. What the reasons might have been will be examined shortly. At the time the proponents of détente had to show that a stabilization of the arms race was in the Soviet interest and that the United States was disposed to co-operate in such a stabilization.

The American signing of the Partial Test Ban Treaty in July, 1963, furnished the necessary reassurance. Although the treaty was confined to testing nuclear weapons, both parties expected that its existence would induce mutual restraint in the expansion of military forces. For a time this was indeed the case.

The course of the negotiation of the Partial Test Ban Treaty illustrates some of the main themes of this essay. Misperception of each other's intentions played a role, and the misperception was heightened by domestic political considerations on each side. But these difficulties were overcome, in my opinion, largely because the terms of coexistence were being negotiated for the first time on the basis of a realistic prognosis of the future; namely, an extended period of over-all American superiority. It was unrealistic to expect a settlement on the basis of parity because ultimately the American electorate would not settle for much less than circumstances required.

The records of the negotiations for the Partial Test Ban Treaty have not been made public and therefore no detailed account of their course is possible. Enough has been revealed, however, to make clear that misperception of the other party's purpose played an important role. The most striking piece of evidence is an interview that Khrushchev gave to Norman Cousins, the editor of *The Saturday Review*, whom Kennedy asked to discover what was holding up the negotiations for a treaty. (The text was published November 7, 1964, only after Khrushchev was dismissed from office.) Khrushchev complained that the United States had behaved in a fashion that furnished ammunition to his critics. The sticking point in the negotiations had become the provisions for monitoring and inspecting underground nuclear tests. Khrushchev maintained that unofficial emissaries of President Kennedy had promised that the United States was prepared to accept a certain number of tests and that the United States had later reneged, insisting on more. This could be interpreted to mean, and some Soviet officials did so interpret it, that the United States was not serious about negotiations, because as soon as the Soviet Union agreed to an offer it was withdrawn. Although Khrushchev did not say so, it was obvious that a test ban treaty with the United States would necessarily entail further aggravation of relations with the Chinese. If the United States was indeed playing at negotiations, the Soviet Union would have to pay the price of worsened relations with the Chinese without achieving a stabilization of the arms race.

The misunderstanding was surmounted (by dropping the projected agreement on underground tests). It had been obvious all along that the United States was more eager than the Soviet Union to conclude a test ban treaty, but not because the United States was more devoted to peace or because she was more concerned about the consequences of a possible nuclear war. The test ban treaty symbolically recognized that the accommodation between the Soviet Union and the

United States would be made on the basis of American superiority. Not surprisingly it was easier for the United States to accept this than for the Soviet Union to relinquish, for a considerable period of time, the hope of being one of the two great powers arranging the affairs of the world.

The Partial Test Ban Treaty marked the beginning of what I have suggested is a period of coexistence different in quality from that which preceded. Since then the terms of coexistence have been undergoing constant modification, as do all political arrangements, and it is not clear at this writing whether the present distinctive phase of coexistence is on the point of termination or whether it will enjoy a longer lease of life without radical alteration. Some of the features of the relationship between the Soviet Union and the United States are relatively fixed and others subject to change. Least subject to alteration, perhaps, is the economic preponderance of the United States.

The almost unbroken economic growth of the United States since 1945 is a remarkable and apparently continuing phenomenon. Soviet economists have now recognized in print that Keynesianism works in the United States. This is not the place to set forth an extensive account of this development but mention of one striking fact might be permitted. American companies wishing to establish large-scale enterprises are often able to borrow the necessary capital from European lending institutions that would not make similar loans to European firms.* A host of factors explains the more favorable prospects of American business, and in combination they seem to point to an increase in the distance be-

* See Leo Model, "The Politics of Private Foreign Investment," *Foreign Affairs,* July, 1967, pp. 639–51; and Jean-Jacques Servan-Schreiber, *Le Defi American* (Paris, 1967).

tween the U.S. economy and its closest competitors. By contrast the Soviet Union is inviting western European business into the Soviet Union. It takes an effort of the imagination, however, to contemplate western European countries offering inducements to the Soviet Union to bring branches of its industrial establishments into their countries in the conviction that Soviet efficiency was superior.

The enormous disparity in economic strength has made it possible for the United States since 1965 to increase its military expenditures by almost half, that is, by some $25 billion a year. This perhaps explains the reason (or rationale) for the Soviet exercise of the option to expand its armed forces. It is therefore meaningful to talk about a new phase of the arms race. From the U.S. point of view the Soviet Union is changing the military relationship in very important areas. When the Partial Test Ban Treaty was signed the United States had roughly four times as many offensive weapons of intercontinental range as the Soviet Union. Now the ratio has been significantly altered; if the Soviet buildup continues at its present rate without any change in the American position, the United States will no longer be superior. Changes in defensive-weapons systems can be viewed as equally disturbing. Although the American technological judgment, as expressed by Secretary of Defense McNamara, is that neither the Soviet Union nor the United States could improve defensive weapons sufficiently to make a retaliatory blow acceptable, the future is nevertheless worrisome because of the uncertainty of technological judgments. Such judgments do not have a reassuring history. Few expected at the inception of its development, for example, that the ICBM would have been so thoroughly perfected in such short order. Reliability and accuracy have far exceeded expectations. The outlook for defensive systems in the late sixties is considerably less favorable than the outlook for the efficiency of offensive systems was in the late fifties, but the uncertainty troubled the American authorities enough to cause them to start a defensive system. McNamara's tone of reluctant necessity in justifying the initial defensive system has produced widespread speculation that the decision was influenced by domestic necessities in an election year when the public-opinion polls showed declining approval of the Johnson administration because of the Vietnamese war. Of course it is not possible to determine how great a role domestic politics plays in such decisions, but its influence in this case seems unmistakable. From the American point of view, the decision to make a thin deployment of defensive missiles seemed a necessary response to the changes in the Soviet military posture. An American spokesman in a candid mood might admit that domestic necessities may have caused the decision to be taken earlier than it might otherwise have been, but he would probably insist that the improvements in the Soviet military posture would sooner or later have made the response necessary.

The Soviet appreciation of the situation is necessarily different. In their view the increase of the American military budget by $25 billion a year created a change in the weapons balance to which they felt required to respond. More often than not in the interaction of the Soviet and American military establishments, one side had responded to improvements by the other with advances in a different weapons system. For example, the Soviet military establishment has always devoted more attention and resources to defense than offense. Sometimes Soviet writers have tried to present this as evidence of Soviet peaceableness in contrast to American aggressiveness, but the situation is more complicated. At the beginning of the arms race the United States conceived its task to be the defense of its allies, most of whom were located within striking distance of the Soviet ground forces. Unwilling and to some extent unable to match Soviet strength in the European theater, the United States improved those systems in which it enjoyed superiority, namely nuclear weapons and aircraft. An offensive force capable of prompt and devastating damage to the Soviet Union was presumed to protect western Europe by deterring the Soviet Union. Thus the United States developed offensive weapons as a deterrent which it automatically characterized as defensive. (Of course the Soviets had to worry that this instrumentality could have been employed offensively, particularly before they had acquired their own long-range nuclear weapons sytems.)

Since at all times, including the present, the Soviet Union has been inferior in nuclear weapons, she never entertained the notion of starting a nuclear war. Given the assumption of American initiation of the war, defensive installations to reduce the damage as much as possible seemed to be justified, and since World War II the proportion of the Soviet military budget devoted to defense has always been higher than that of the United States. This rather familiar ground has been retraversed to establish the background for the present Soviet decision to emphasize ballistic missile defense. The United States has recently made enormous improvements in its ground forces and the supporting systems necessary to deploy them all over the world. Given the long American naval and amphibious experience, it would probably take ten years for the Soviet Union to match that capability, assuming comparable economic resources and naval bases. It is not necessary to elaborate the comparison further to establish that the Soviet Union could not expect to correct what it considered an imbalance in an area in which the United States had the advantages of experience, a long lead, and greater resources. Moreover, the naval and the amphibious elements in the Soviet military establishment probably had the least specific political weight in the struggle for the resources alloted to the whole military establishment. Therefore both the habit of favoring the defense and the hopes of surpassing the United States in a new weapons system combined to produce the decision to go ahead with defensive-weapons systems.

Since large shifts in military posture are made in increments, it is possible that despite the momentum of their own that such investments generate, the Soviet Union and the United States will break off such a deployment before it reaches its potential. Such a desirable outcome would, if the above analysis has any validity, depend on the removal of the disturbance to the system which has precipitated the new cycle of the arms race—namely, the Vietnamese war and the expansion it has required.

As in the United States, the Soviet decision to depart from the spirit of the Partial Test Ban Treaty was made within the context of a domestic political struggle. The evidence of controversy in the Soviet Union on the technological outlook for a defense against missiles and on the wisdom of deploying it is unmistakable. We can, again, only isolate the various forces at play in the resolution of the controversy without being able to determine their relative importance.

In some ways the Vietnamese war has been an even greater trial for the Soviet Union than for the United

States.* The Soviet Union has been unwilling or unable
to offer effective assistance to another socialist country
that has been under U.S. attack from the air since Feb-
ruary, 1965. Nor has the Soviet Union been able to prevail upon the United States to stop the bombing so that
peace negotiations might have a better chance of going
forward. Nor has the Soviet Union been able to prevail
upon the North Vietnamese to start negotiating with
the United States before the cessation of bombing. The
Soviet Union is impotent and helpless to influence
events, and the cost to her prestige in other socialist
countries has been heavy.

It is instructive that even when the Soviet Union is
suffering such serious political damage from the United
States, and some officials in the Soviet Union believe
that this is a major motivation of the United States, it
still does not abandon the hope of improved relations
with the United States. We can only speculate on the
reasons. The Soviet Union may hope that the United
States will quit the war as popular opposition mounts
and that then something like the former situation can
be restored. She may expect that the North Vietnamese
will decide to negotiate rather than continue the struggle. But these hopeful projections of the future do not
seem to explain the tenacity with which the Soviet
Union keeps the door open for better relations with the
United States after the conclusion of the Vietnamese
war. Apparently some political groups in the Soviet
Union have developed a vested interest in good relations
because they permit more support for domestic Soviet

---

* In another place [*Intervention Against Communism* (The
Johns Hopkins University Press, 1967)] I have argued that the
Vietnamese war is a mistake from the point of view of American
interests. Here attention is confined to its role in the relations
between the Soviet Union and the United States.

programs. Otherwise the Soviet Union would probably be more tempted to lead a world peace movement to condemn "American aggression in Vietnam." U.S. policy has so few defenders abroad that such a Soviet effort would probably yield easy and prompt successes. But the détente-oriented forces, although able to keep the door open for an improvement in American-Soviet relations, were apparently unable to stop the allocation of funds to ballistic missile defense.

Should the arms race indeed enter a new spiral, the détente ushered in by the Partial Test Ban Treaty will not have been the beginning of a period in which the area of coincidence of interest between the Soviet Union and the United States was progressively extended. Instead, the pattern of relations may be that of alternate contraction and expansion of the number of issues in which the two parties discern a community of interests. This represents a more limited hope for the future than that current at the conclusion of the Partial Test Ban Treaty, namely, that relations would improve with few if any interludes of retrogression. Nevertheless the present chastened mood is still qualitatively different from that of the cold war, when progressive deterioration was assumed. The hope that tomorrow, or the day after tomorrow, may be better increases tolerance on both sides and reduces the misunderstandings produced by misperception. For example, although some in the Soviet Union seem to believe that Vietnam is the first in a series of American interventions, others hope that similar interventions will not take place and therefore refrain from destroying channels of communication which may serve in the future. The United States adopts the same attitude toward the significant and growing Soviet contribution to the North Vietnamese defense. During the cold war the United States would probably have taxed the Soviet authorities with prolonging the war by helping the North Vietnamese, while the Soviet authorities would probably have organized international protest against the attack on a socialist state.

The two parties approach each other much more carefully in the conviction that established patterns of co-operation are worth maintaining, while still viewing each other as antagonists. Although the Soviet leaders have accepted the reality of growing American power and therefore have had to postpone the date of the ultimate demise of capitalism, its ultimate disappearance is still an article of faith. Coexistence, as always, still means coexistence *until* or coexistence *while*—that is, coexistence until capitalism becomes weaker, until the Soviet Union becomes stronger, while the contradictions of capitalism are undermining its foundations, and while the preconditions for socialism are being established in the third world. After all, if the two systems are to coexist indefinitely, the term coexistence is not necessary.

Those who want to keep their faith look for and find evidence to support it. From the Soviet point of view, and not only the Soviet point of view, the United States seems to be facing its greatest crises at the height of its material power. The American racial crisis is perhaps the most serious domestic crisis since the Civil War. To the Soviets the Vietnamese war is but another example of the flaws inherent in the capitalist system. The United States cannot conclude a war whose dimensions, duration, and political costs continue to mount far beyond what was anticipated. If the American dilemma is to be explained by the inability to preserve the proper proportion between ends and means, that is enough to feed Soviet confidence in the future, since it is likely, whatever its outcome, that the experience of the Vietnamese war will reduce public and congressional support for all kinds of American involvement in foreign affairs. The prospect is even more gloomy or promising, depending on one's position, if the United States with a prevision of the course of events has embroiled itself in a morass from which no exit is in sight at the present writing.

Such events naturally nourish the Soviet hope that capitalism is doomed despite its power and rapid growth. This faith limits the scope of even temporary accommodations on the basis of coincidence of interests, because the Soviet Union must weigh the short-run convenience of such an arrangement against its tendency to arrest the deterioration of the capitalist system. If the ideological component had ceased to play any role in Soviet thinking, the obvious course would be to scale down the arms race and employ the resources thus saved elsewhere. After all, no important territorial questions are any longer at issue. But the Soviet Union does not yet seem quite ready to settle for the role of tending its own garden. The renewal of her investment in the Near East after a serious reverse is the most recent example of continued commitment to the goals of a great power with overseas interests.

When the Soviet Union was at its weakest fifty years ago, capitalism was expected to founder in important European states. Soviet expectations about the future and vitality of capitalism have changed markedly since then, but the time has not yet come when the indefinite existence of capitalism is accepted. Perhaps this basic tenet of Marxism is now being revised, but until it is, the Soviet Union can only view coexistence as a transitional stage.